Treasures OF THE Journey

Treasures OF THE Journey

Awakening Feminine Wisdom, Beauty & Passion

CORVUS
PRESS

www.corvuspress.com

Copyright © 2012 by Fran Clarke

Published by Corvus Press
P.O. Box 2597
Lafayette, LA, 70502
Email: info@corvuspress.com
www.corvuspress.com

• Editorial & Production: Jane Blunschi & Angelina Leger, Lafayette, LA
• Cover & Interior Design: Angelina Leger, Lafayette, LA
• Photography: Jason Cohen, Lafayette, LA
• Submissions & interviews transcribed by Tammy Labiche, Lafayette, LA

ISBN-13: 978-0-9829239-9-3
Printed by Lightning Source, US

ACKNOWLEDGEMENTS

A wonderful group of people contributed to making this book the best it could be, and I offer my sincere gratitude to all of them.

My phenomenal children, Chelsea and Michael, for your love and support. You are bright sparks in this world!

My amazing circle of friends for their love and support – it means the world to me.

The community at Corvus Press: Jeremy Broussard, Founder; Jane Blunschi, Publisher; and Angelina Leger, Art Director, for guiding this work and making it a reality.

Jason Cohen for capturing the unique spirit of each woman through the lens of his camera.

Tammy LaBiche for transcribing all the poetry, testimonials and interviews.

– F.C.

*This book is dedicated to the women who have been
a part of my journey and calling.*

*My women ancestors, whose shoulders I stand on, and all
the teachers in my life for their guidance and wisdom.*

*The ordinary extraordinary women of Heroine's Journey circles, for
placing your trust in me. What an honor it is to walk alongside you!*

*The amazing Heroines who share their treasures of the journey in
the pages of this book. You are mentors to other women.*

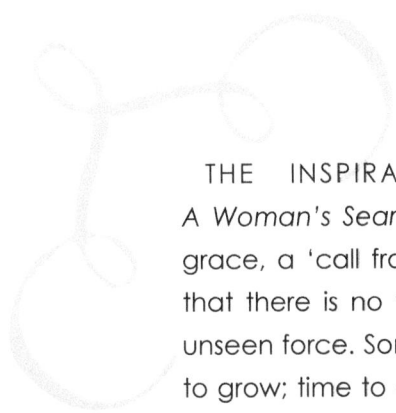

THE INSPIRATION FOR *The Heroine's Journey: A Woman's Search for Truth* came through a moment of grace, a 'call from my soul.' When this happens, I know that there is no turning back. I am pulled forward by an unseen force. Something deep inside knows when it is time to grow; time to confront and loosen the constrictions that are holding us back and keeping us feeling small; time to inhabit the greater potential of who we came here to be.

According to mythology, when the Heroine says, Yes! to the 'Call' she steps over a threshold and enters unfamiliar territory. This was true for me and for the extraordinary women you will meet on these pages. They are some of the participants of *The Heroine's Journey* program.

When I first developed *The Heroine's Journey*, I could never have imagined the holiness that I would experience through the unfolding of beauty, spirit and power of the women in each circle. Like precious buds unfolding to reveal their exquisite innate natures, these women committed to a process of becoming themselves – each one unique, each one aligning with personal truth. When that happens, joy flows forth, peace prevails, personal relationships are governed by respect and integrity, and creativity flourishes.

This is what you will observe as you meet the Heroines on these pages. Their words reveal much about their journey, about themselves. Most of them had never written before participating in this program, but were able to access and express from deep within.

I invite you to meet these amazing women!

I am strong

I am creative and capable.
I respect the wisdom that is continuously gifted to me.
I strive to live in honor and gratitude for all that is given.

I speak simply and clearly from a place of truth.
I love intimately and passionately and sometimes from a distance.
I desire to relinquish my fears and attachment to outcomes.

I continue to become more and more aware — thus my life expands.
I trust that my transition into forever life will simply and incredibly
be a full receptivity and awareness of the Divine's creation.
I give generously and express gratitude.

I manifest abundance in my life.
I honor and trust the Sacred, the Divine, the Holy Mystery.

I innocently delight in seeing a robin.

I choose to contain, to nurture and to be with the experiences of my life
until it is time to release them.
I am becoming more fully the woman God intended.
I believe in miracles that allow me to grow through and past pain,
into an experience that is rich and blessed.

I wish to live with joy and delight, curiosity and imagination,
freedom and peace.
I believe my life, my love, my relationships flow into forever.
I desire to become more spontaneous and free spirited,
I am strong and warm and kind.

– *Cheryl Guidry*

Cheryl Guidry

Katherine Vincent-Istre

Sands of time

Each grain holds moments in my life
Grains of happiness and sadness
Grasping the sand I close my eyes
I hear the ocean and smell the salt
With each grain moving and changing
Opportunities open
Squeezing out negative old habits and
Escaping shackles
I place my foot into the sand
Wiggle my toes and step into a
New awareness of a rebirth
Of myself.

– Kathryn Vincent-Istre

Tension of Change

Hate It
Love It
Move thru It
Never know what's after It
Never know what Change brings
Stay in the flow ∞

– Tammy Labiche Henley

The Divine Spark is Born

Void.
Emptiness which shrouds potential.
The dark comes alive with fire,
    electricity, creativity.
Sparks of the Divine fly with abandon.
And yet with Purpose.
We each get a spark.
We each also get a place of void.

– Virginia Webb

Virginia Webb

"Out of the believer's heart shall flow rivers of living water." John 7:38

Birth to Myself

Conceived from the thoughts of others,
I start to form into what someone else has determined I will be.

The voices of the outside world, barely audible,
will soon shatter my quiet world with loud opinions and forceful beliefs.

The time has come. I am pushed out into the world unknown.
I follow, obediently.
I think, thoughts not my own.
I accept, the unacceptable.
I live life, for someone else.

Weak and fragile,
I succumb.

I claim the life someone else has chosen for me.
And soon, I become, who they think, I should be.

I tolerate,
am forced to,
put up with,
fall victim to,
my life.

Until, I question:
Who it is I want to be.
Who it is I know I am.

Then, I start to form and grow,
into what it is I determine I want to be.

My voice, now the only one audible,
shatters their beliefs.

I step out into the unknown,
strong and determined.

Reclaiming what is mine:
I inhabit,
have a place,
hold strong,
take control
of my life.

> Born again,
>   I give birth to Myself

– Kandise France

My Pilgrimage

Bend the rules

Push aside the obstacles

Reach beyond

Stretch and Grow

Shake it off

Feel the Movement

Feel the Freedom

Feel the weightless LEAP

– Robin Harbourt

Bessie Senette

In Between

Secret and silent,
Betrayed and lied to,
I nurse my domesticated emotions.

Soft-stepping defensiveness
Limiting my integrity,
I silently seethe.

Who am I?
How in the hell would I know?
I have danced so far from
My original face.

Side stepping, tip toeing, spinning in place,
Surviving, not thriving,
Bending the limits of my psyche.

A frozen river of rage lives deep inside me.
Is it capable of violence? Indeed!
But so far it ravages only me.

Why shouldn't it?
I am the one guilty of abandoning the star child;
Denying her safety, aborting her dreams.

Yes, she was abused by others
But forgotten by me.
Lost in her tortured loneliness, she sleeps.

Who will give her vindication, if not me?
I alone know her stilled voice
I alone know her story.

Only now, so much later
Have I begun to defend her holy ground,
Singing her back to sacred heart.

A gentle cooing restoring Eve's Faith,
Blossoming slowly, the lotus opens
to reveal once again her original face.

Sensing touch as love's power,
we remember together
a long lost radiant strength.

In my acceptance and understanding
She will live free,
Unwilling now or ever again to sacrifice

Herself on the altar of your need.

– Bessie Senette

Brittany Broussard

*T*he idea for this piece came to me long before it was created. I would think about it on occasion, cultivate what process I would use to make it a reality. And then one day it came to life. On a day that I poured, literally poured, my past existence dripping across an off-white painted board.

I was searching for a true meaning of life, a way of being that felt natural and real. I started *The Heroine's Journey* after two years of searching, getting a small little taste of what was genuine to me. Once my journey started, it was mind blowing, the work encouraged me to move light years ahead. To let go of past expectations and live from my heart. It was a hard-hitting process, both in sessions and in my everyday life. Then, one day I took a drive to Lake Martin, wrote my first song, and knew from that moment I was a different person in the best way possible. I finally knew what was authentic for me. I immediately gathered the items needed for my vision. I was so inspired; it felt like I was floating. As I poured paint down this large board, I literally felt myself let go of my "past life."

– Brittany Broussard

Released

A body prone vibrates to the rhythm . . .

Drums, yes.

Thank God for the drums!

My core center pulsing.

My back receiving the life breath.

My stomach open.

My heart follows in all directions.

Two hands appear, wrapped together like a butterfly.

Shame drips down my face,

opening the gates at my throat,

exiting my shoulders

into my lymph centers

and out of my hands.

My Madonna receiving reds, yellows, and oranges.

Warmth at my throat sliding down

Tying the bow of the child

there is a wing attached

a butterfly angel closes her eyes and sleeps.

– Stephanie McCullor

Stephanie McCullor

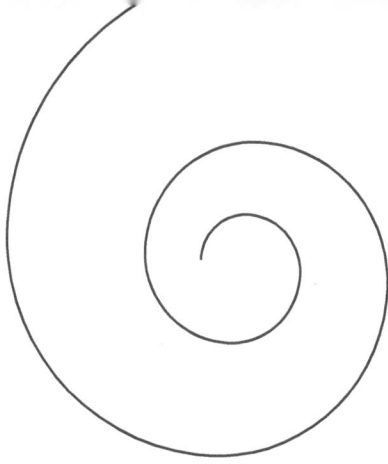

The name of the piece is "Stage 0" in honor of the concept associated with this "Beginning before Beginnings" stage. It came out of a visual I received while participating in the music mediation on that day's step in the Journey.

The piece illustrates the interconnectedness of spirit (the linking of multicolored hearts) and how spirit is interwoven through and before manifestation (the never ending spiral/ helix). It brings me comfort because it reminds me that when I allow myself to meet others heart to heart (as challenging as it is sometimes) I reaffirm my connection to humanity and to the sacred. When I look at it now I usually think, "Damn, the inspiration was flowing that day!" because I hadn't painted for years before that and I haven't painted since. Thank you for helping make that possible.

I have learned that I have unwavering personal needs and deep rooted insecurities, both of which deserve and demand my attention and care, and that I need to address them with love and patience.

I have learned that the Universe speaks in subtle but consistent ways.

I have learned that when I get frustrated or angry at someone's words or actions, it's ok to address it, and most of the time it really is them, not me.

I have learned that my intuition is right 98% of the time and to go with it!

I have learned that asking for help is the hardest thing to do but it is made easier by knowing strong women who have gone through whatever I have before me.

– Helen Osterhold

Choices

I lay down in the surf.
The waves of the Ocean encompass me.
I allow myself to feel the soft sand beneath me.
I am very conscious of the flow of water that
covers my body.
It is somehow a cleansing sort of feeling.
A shedding of the outer layer of my soul...

I begin to sit erect and look out into the endless sea.
I feel a sense of security being close to the ocean.
It empowers me.
It is a place where my soul feels at home.
I get my strength there.

I return with a renewed strength to make choices in my life.
What a powerful concept.
The act of choosing can be very liberating.

So many times, in my life and yours, we forego our
ability to choose, mostly because the fear of making
the wrong choice overcomes
our confidence to even make one.

Choices that involve only my influence, my spirit,
no opinions from others, no other pressure.
I can honestly say that I believed every choice I made
was by me, and for me, but the truth is, very few were.
I know that now, the ones that are the closest to my
heart are the ones made by the heroine in me.
It is only now that I have the courage to choose
without hesitation, doubt, or influence.

What a wonderful feeling.
A true heroine makes her own choices.

– Karen Durio

Karen Durio

Alyce Wise

Life Art

You are the medium
You are the medium that goes
    on smoothly or clumps on the canvas
You are the medium that creates
     the colors you desire
You are the medium that creates
      the magnificent, joyful art that
      is your life
Your thoughts
Your responses
Your actions
Your words
Your relating
That is your palate.
It is your artwork, your painting
Your book, your sculpture,
Your dance and you are the medium.

– Alyce Wise

Kathy Dumesnil

Fragmentation

This piece of art, called "Mythos" continues to be a source of inspiration and connection of my own belonging to nature, self and the collective. Upon its completion, my response was "Where did this come from?" Now 10 months later of "being" with this painting, my perspective has continually shifted. I am changing as I believe the painting is communicating that I am birthing myself.

Birthing an open heartedness . . . finding a place, a nest to nurture myself, learning kindness and stillness of heart. Seeing all the fragments of myself with equanimity. The bird seems to hold a vision, is the connection to spirit which is my guide to inner wisdom.

Within the creative process of *The Heroine's Journey*, the MARI cards, visualizations, writing and art, I was empowered and found meaning through self discovery.

Being a seeker of my own authentic self, "being" an artist is what I know now is my purpose.

In the process, a knowing deep within me acknowledged that the creative longing had been fractured and was now awakened. Along with much undertow and turbulence I am still evolving but my heart and soul have connected in rhythm.

– Kathy Dumesnil

Denise Thibodeaux

The Heroine's Journey cast an initiating light on a source of love and power that I continually draw from. My outer world would look very different if I had not taken that crucial journey with Fran into the inner worlds. The courage I gained from that passage gave me the confidence to open my eyes to possibilities I hadn't seen before, to say yes to those opportunities, and to watch them become realities I might have only dreamed of.

– *Denise Thibodeaux*

Fragmenting, suffering, unfolding
As the soul breaks through
Anticipating, initiating, awaiting
The birth of the new

Orphaned dreams awakened
Illusions of fears uncovered
Sisters, daughters, mothers, women
Taking back the silence of each other

– *Katherine Moody McCormick*

The Seer

Come. And tell me, Sister
In that singsong voice
In the octave beyond the man-ear
Chant out your secrets
Whisper the way out of shame
For the waters are high
And this river is wide
And I've got little ones, weak ones in my charge
Teach me Sister the she-laws
I hear we all go together or none at all
I hear we are more powerful than the sun
I hear we are the true life-force in this world
But I've been taught to fear
To fear myself, to fear you
And your wild woman eyes
Where I see myself
The one I was born as
The one I must return to
Deep in my earth-child nature
I know the truth
My mother bore me from the soil
Ripe with power and potential
Ripe with strength and stamina
My birthright stolen on my very first night
A ritual theft of myself
While my mother slept the peaceful sleep
Of a woman too long in this man's world

– *Jessica Breaux*

I am
my own
heroine

Jessica Breaux

Jessica Wiley

To "flower my true self"

Prior to *The Heroine's Journey* — one year prior — I had drawn an abstract picture with this layered bulb. Later through the journey, I would learn what that meant for me . . .

Most of my work started to develop in the later stages. I believe I had anger at that time due to my repression of who I truly was. I titled Stage 11 Flamed in the midst of burning.

I visualized that I was hanging upside down on a stage and my hair caught fire. But I bloomed. Profound experience. A group member later directed me to the tarot card with the upside down card and it matched exactly what I felt and was experiencing.

Flamed in the midst of burning

Your words were
smothering blankets
darting daggers
of toxic rain

Embers did not engulf
flame licks intensified
but you flowered me
and showed me
how I do want to live
by experiencing how I did not

– Jessica Wiley

Life

With feet now firmly planted in the earth,
I am well into my journey,
Hesitant at first, one slow sure step then another.
Breathe in, breathe out, Feel the dirt between my toes
and the vibration of the world around me.
Head held high, feeling the confidence all around me
like a warm breeze thru my hair.
Breathe in, breathe out, life is here,
now grab it and run.
It is mine to have.

– Lorie Duval

Lorie Duval

My soul is my own

My soul is my own, it's not yours
You do not own it, you cannot claim it.
It's mine.

You live your life in your small, safe, little box.
Fear grips you, paralyzes you, keeps you there.
That is your life, not mine.
I won't join you there.

Your anger is yours, I don't want it!!
The screaming, criticisms, judgments—All of it.
That is who you are. Not me!
I'm not you.

My journey is to love me, to be my own mother.
My path is not yours and it never will be.
I am not you, I don't want to be you.
I now have the power to embrace me, to love me.
To accept me for who I am, faults, imperfections and all.

I am me.
I am not you

My soul is my own

– Carmen Vidrine

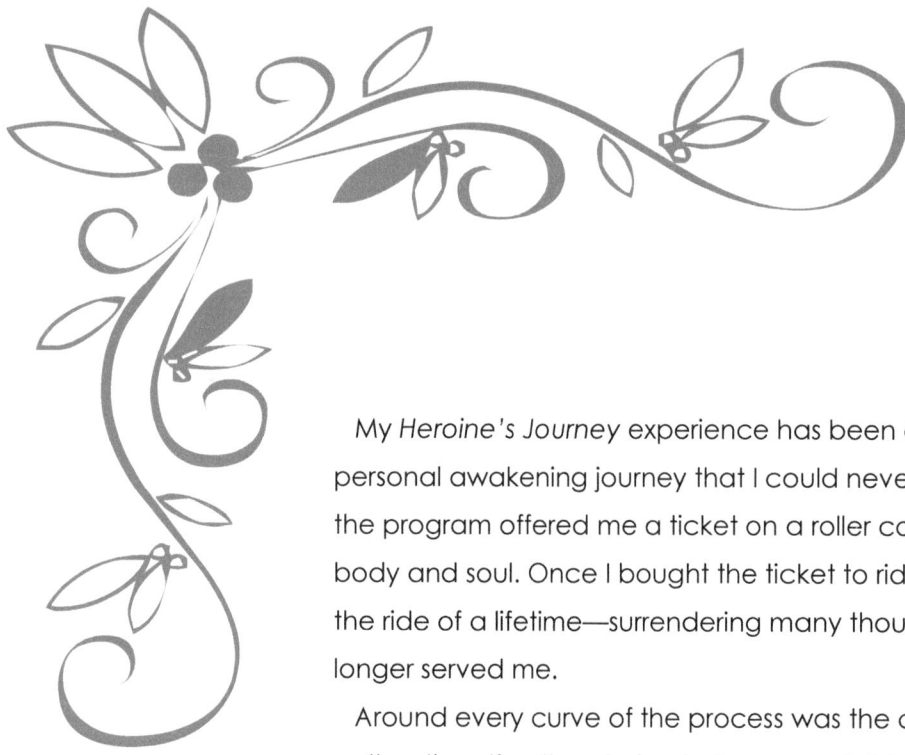

My *Heroine's Journey* experience has been an eye opening, heart jolting and personal awakening journey that I could never have imagined. Each stage of the program offered me a ticket on a roller coaster ride that engaged me, mind, body and soul. Once I bought the ticket to ride—I held on and quickly started the ride of a lifetime—surrendering many thoughts and many patterns that no longer served me.

Around every curve of the process was the choice of choosing to honor my authentic self or the choice to be acceptable to others for comfort and security.

Learning to say 'NO' was a monumental achievement for me because it opened a space within for my personal inner passions to say 'YES' and not feel as though I was an uncaring person.

My Heroine sisters and the individual work of the protocol taught me how to give myself permission to put myself first and that growth and change was not only empowering, but necessary!

A need to surrender was inevitable, and my journey's facilitator and sisters helped me push through the darkness, individuation and growth.

The Heroine's Journey came into my life as I hesitantly said 'Yes' to the ride and it laid a foundation to withstand the bumps, emotional demands and difficult decisions that allowed me to stay the course of self-discovery that continues to this day.

I feel a sense of triumph and confidence to continue to trust the process that *The Heroine's Journey* graciously taught me, and the courage to fearlessly move through life knowing of my personal empowerment. With that knowledge, I am never alone and always ready to learn and move forward. For this, I am grateful to God, Fran and my Heroine sisters!

– Linda Lolan

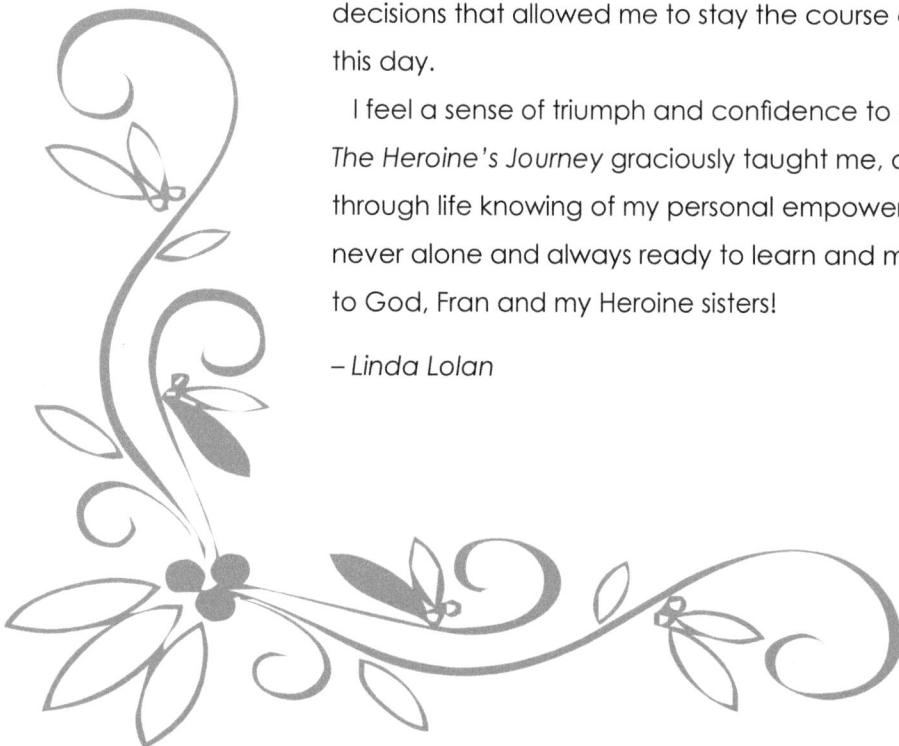

Linda Lolan

Debra Crowe

The Quest

Be present, Stay present, Breathe
Show up for the friend across the circle
She has shown up for you

She suffers, I suffer
She laughs, I dance
She cries, I hug
She is angry, I understand
She is listening, I am grateful
She shows up, I step out

Honor the process of the journey
We are where we are — only this
No recriminating past or fallacy filled future dictates my mood

The journey is through chatter to powerful spaciousness
Space for creativity to flourish — to release a lifetime of apology
Space to sing off key — to open doors closed long ago by casual
criticism that I have repeated to myself for years
Safe space to cradle my Spirit tenderly
I step forward
Flourish on the journey
Laugh, scream, breathe
Breathe
Show up

– Debra Crowe

I Am Here

I AM HERE! NOTICE ME! FEEL ME! EMBRACE ME!

Stripped of all that is confining – inside and outside
Dance around the fire that lies within your soul

Enjoy Me — Celebrate Me — Take Me In

Release those shackles you have placed across your hands – the ropes that bind your eyes from seeing –
the shield that keeps your heart from feeling and the fear that stops your soul from being.
Release the shame, release the fear

EMBRACE ME! FEEL ME! EMBODY ME!

FEEL my skin — HOT — SMOOTH — radiating heat from every pore

FEEL me — embrace me — sing with me — move with me — walk with me — dance with me —
Strip yourself of all that holds you down

Sway your hips to the beat of the drums — FEEL my fire burning in your blood — FEEL my call to be one with
you — to be known — to be experienced

Dance by the light of our fire – open to all that comes our way
Throw away all that is old
It is of no use to you anymore

I AM HERE! FEEL ME! ENJOY ME!
Let me seduce you into your life

Embrace my freedom — embrace my sensuality — FEEL me — I AM HERE!

Let us create our dance — a dance of joy- being one with each other

Sway your hips like so . . . Move your shoulders from side to side . . .
FEEL the beat of the drum.
Can you hear it?! I can! It beats in my soul. It radiates throughout my body.
The vibration is intoxicating.

I AM HERE! FEEL ME! I AM ALIVE!

Run your hands through your hair. FEEL the soft silk of it across your hand.
FEEL the wind and heat radiate across your naked flesh.

Sway into it — lay into it — Take it into your core because that is where I am.

FEEL ME! EMBRACE ME! I AM HERE!
Share me with those you love. Strip yourself of all that holds you back

Dance by our light. Sway to the beat of our song. FEEL the heat of our fire.

That's right . . . Move your hips back and forth . . . Side to side...
The drums pulsate throughout our body . . .
DO NOT BE AFRAID . . . DO NOT FEEL ASHAMED . . .

I LIVE . . .

EMBRACE ME! FEEL ME! I AM HERE!

– Traci Voisine

Traci Voisine

Buried Authenticity

I am excavating history,
Sifting through feminine submissive thoughts.
Reexamining culture, experiences, family and faith
Revealing layer upon layer within me.
My neglected core is unrecognizable — even to me.
Yet, I am nurtured by the heroines that surround me,
Mothers, sisters, friends, daughters — heroines all.
I have excavated the sarcophagus within
and am discovering my authentic self.

– Beverly Breaux

Beverly Breaux

Hamster, hamster on the wheel, ask myself what I feel!

Faster and faster spinning out of control, trying to mend the girl whose story I hold.

Never ever stopping to touch the ground, not expecting enough of the world around.

Always chasing approval from the things that have been, turn to myself and be my own friend.

Accept the things that I see, such a worthy person, that IS me.

I am perfectly imperfect in every way, that's the new deal, and it's OK!

– Lauren Dupre

Lauren Drupre

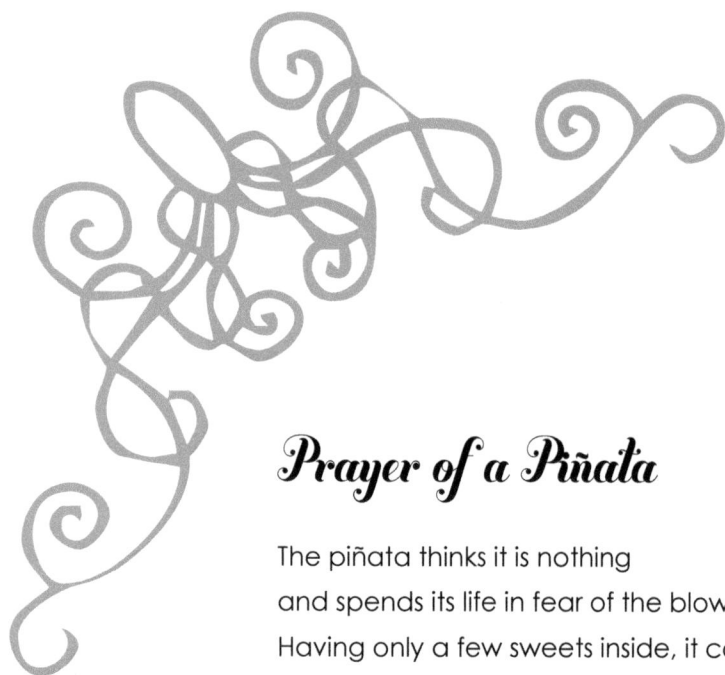

Prayer of a Piñata

The piñata thinks it is nothing
and spends its life in fear of the blow that will break it open.
Having only a few sweets inside, it cannot afford to be broken-open.

Adding more layers to the outside for protection, the piñata said a prayer:
O God, I am afraid to be opened.
A small hole of prayer accidentally lets air come inside
Bringing lightness the piñata had never felt before.

What if — the hole was larger?
Now, the wind blows where it will;
The piñata sighs and rests on the lift of the air-currents.
What a glorious life — not to have to hold on anymore.

– Betty Landreneau

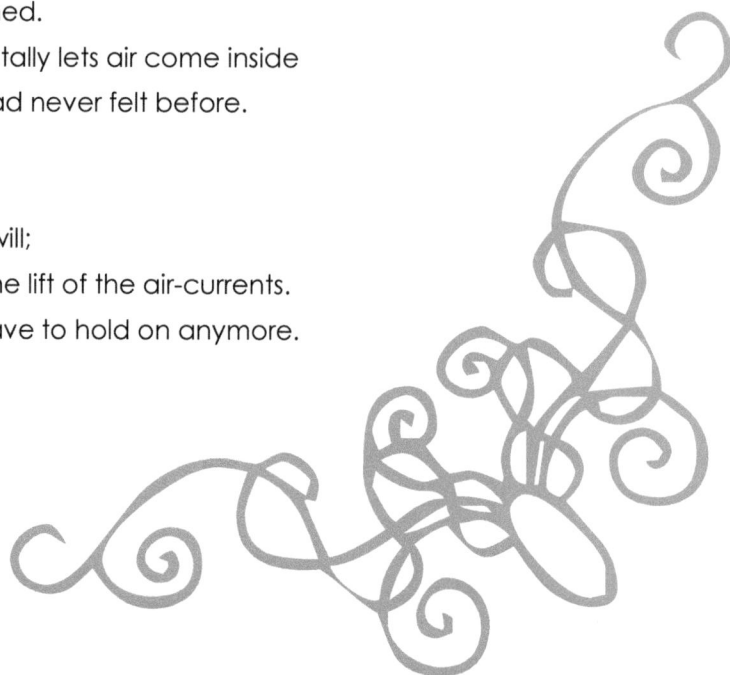

Betty Landreneau

Rain, storm, tornado
flooded streets
A life time washed away
Catch the lifeline
It is there closer than you think
Grab it and enjoy release of a life
To only be baptized in a new one.

– *Joan Livaccari*

True

Nature of Mind
Nature of Heart
What is it that exists
beyond death?
That exists before life?

I told myself

Look within
Do not be afraid
of the dark
There is no such
thing as madness
All illusions fall away

Bridge or Home?

They are one
and the same
Connections uniting
Enveloping
Sustaining
The space between
All belngs
Bridge or Home.

– Adrianne Smith

Denise Marceaux

Struggle – Energy – Free

The only girl on the block
How terrible it was.
The boys were boys
Not interested in having me tag along.
It was always a struggle.
It made me mad
Mad at myself for being a girl.
I had the energy.
I could do anything.
It took me a while
But now I'm free.
Free to do what I want
and the boys tag along.

– Denise Marceaux

Blackened sky, tousled leaves
The sizzle and steam of drops on the pavement.
In a moment of frozen indecision,
The spirit child emerges, separates, skips
Chases the breeze through the shadowed streets.
A crescendo of drumbeats on rooftops and hoods
Quickening, pounding, retreating, fading.
She hopscotches back to her place within
Bringing with her a flood of joy.

– Angie D. Broussard

Angie D. Broussard

There is so much power in one thought.

The power to heal the fastest cancer.

The power to create the deepest,
blackest hole of depression!

The power to raise the vibration
of an entire nation!

The power to calm the smallest fear!

– *Lori Cambre*

In the vast space of uncolored universe . . .
The bluegreen Orb calls
Its white light glows, oceans
        dance and lava flows.
Ecstatic, oozing life
    Moves
            Radiating
                    Pulsing
                            Rolling
                                    Roaring
            1 RIDE.

A light beams . . .
All stare. . .   Waiting
            I'm PATIENT
Dancing light disappoints.

Waters flood in
    Then no one waits
No eyes   No ears
        No stares
The rhythm of water sloshes
    In and out   and wears away
JUDGEMENT
                    A softer exterior
                    A stronger center appears

– Joy Merino

Hallelujah River

My song is a river
Humble beginnings,
Conceived in a secret, sacred space
Within — from a source never without

A slow, steady trickle gives way
to a flowing stream
Gently caressing my spirit,
lapping at my soul
Offering refuge in snakelike twists and turns

Then, it roars
Drowning soothing reminders of
peace and relaxation
As its waterfall reveals itself,
BEHOLD — the unexpected release
of unseen power

Riding on its rapids
A rush of adventure awakens me
Digging a deep path within
Peeling layer after layer, creating
cavernous canyons
At unreachable depths

Running dry at times, overflowing at others
Ever-changing
Life-giving
Life-threatening
Always summoning wonder and awe,
Ever-connected to its faithful source
Its mouth ever singing Hallelujah

– Melanie Pharr

Melanie Pharr

Shala Fontenot

The Heroine's Journey for me was a grace in motion! I have experienced many different workshops and other modalities, all that I am grateful for, but *The Heroine's Journey* was the anchor and umbrella of something even larger. For me, it was poetry, art, music all mixed together in a very organic way that continues to pave a road of freedom and self-realization. I am humbled and grateful for the co-creation of my life and the gift of my experience with the work of *The Heroine's Journey* that continues to unfold in many different aspects. It has opened a doorway for me to experience the breath of life in so many beautiful ways.

– Shala Fontenot

In Search of Essence

I AM A WOMAN OF MANY YEARS
A WOMAN OF MANY TEARS

LONG HAVE I LIVED

WHEN TIME WAS NOT OF ESSENCE
I WAS BORN OF AN ANCIENT SPIRIT

FOR I HEAR THE POUNDING OF THUNDER
IN THE DRUM OF MY HEART

I AM A WOMAN OF MANY YEARS
A WOMAN OF MANY TEARS

LONG HAVE I LIVED

– Harriet Taylor

Harriet Taylor

Betty Mattiza

WHO IS THIS WOMAN

WHO AM I

THIS WOMAN OF ADVANCING YEARS

WHERE AM I GOING

WHERE IS THE GATEWAY TO LIFE

THE WAY TO PRIDE AND FULFILMENT

THE ANSWERS TO THIS YEARNING

WHO AM I

– Betty Mattiza

Jany Champagne

The Photograph

One look, held . . . and captured
by the beauty of your face
I am drawn . . .

As the waters of your memory
stir, I feel a gentle, steady
current of your presence within
me.

My heart grieves for unmade
connections, and it delights with
honor in reaching for you now.

The warmth of your Spirit
baptizes the orphaned parts
of me in belonging.

Your energy washes
over me . . . I belong

– Jany Champagne

Written in November, 2004, about my maternal grandmother from Scotland and the intense connection I made with her during The Heroine's Journey *process. She passed on in 1989.*

Determination

Loneliness

Desperation

Hesitation

Confidence

Fear

Frustration

Love

Power

The inspiration for these self-photographs came through my experience while participating in *The Heroine's Journey*. Following the call of my creative instinct, I hesitantly shared them with my group. I was amazed at their reaction! Their encouragement allowed this and other passions to arise. Now, I have taken bigger risks to follow my dreams, and I continue to be amazed and in awe of it all.

– *Silvia Bertolazzi*

Silvia Bertolazzi

Lori Henderson

My body expresses the
battleground of coping in relationships

Toxic tension of blind color and pain

To feel powerless and let
anger surface from below

My own hidden needs that parents
couldn't give are received from deep within

My voice remembers
and feels the charge of self love

– Lori Henderson

I FULLY EMBRACE MY DIVINE ROLE AS NURTURER, ADVOCATE, FACILITATOR, WARRIOR, AND CONDUIT OF LOVE FOR THE TRUE VICTIMS OF THE WORLD: ABUSED AND NEGLECTED ANIMALS AND PEOPLE. I WILL EMBODY THE BELIEF THAT ALL LIFE MATTERS AND IS SACRED. I WILL DO THIS WITHOUT HESITATION OR APOLOGY. I WILL FEEL GENTLE, YET POWERFUL, AS I LIVE MY LIFE'S PURPOSE: RADIATING LOVE, KINDNESS AND COMPASSION INTO THE WORLD. LIVING IN THIS WAY WILL STRENGTHEN MY DIVINE CONNECTION TO OUR CREATOR AND ALL LIVING BEINGS SHARING OUR PLANET. WITHIN ME LIE ALL THE SKILLS, ABILITIES, AND RESOURCES REQUIRED TO CREATE A FULFILLING AND POWERFUL LIFE AND TO FACILITATE OTHERS TO DO THE SAME.

– *Katharine Porter*

Katharine Porter

Mary Lee Fontenot

Born to Give

Born to give, born to share, a spirit of hope
and faith, fractured for a time, searching
for miracles, a new life is born!

Born to learn, born to give openly,
searching for truth, direction, love given,
love received, warm embraces secure the
beauty that lies ahead!

– Mary Lee Fontenot

The Moon

The moon speaks to me
        Through the branch
        Of the backyard oak
        It says …
You and I are 1
        Timeless
Not like the cloud.

– *Toni Daigre*

Toni Daigre

As I looked at my drawings that I had made in the year I did the program, I was amazed to see the movement. I had arrived at a place in my life that felt right. I had regained my ease in living life again.

– Linda Christian

Linda Christian

Where do I begin to say what all The Heroine's Journey has done for me?

It has given me a voice.

It has taught me how to write poetry.

It has given me great friendships.

It has facilitated my creativity.

It has taught me to sit with the feelings.

It has given me COURAGE: the courage to speak, to reach out, to try new things, to apologize when I'm wrong and to not apologize when I'm not wrong.

It has brought my SMILE back along with LAUGHTER.

Thank you for making Heroine's Journey available. I'm sure it has saved lives and made many lives more abundant.

Things I have done since beginning *The Heroine's Journey*:

Learned to quilt and have sewn many quilts.

Started teaching piano lessons.

Began writing poetry and took poetry workshops.

Began playing djembe drums and took classes. Also quilted drum head covers.

Began taking photographs.

Wrote a book of photography and poetry. (Super Sighted)

Have an exhibit at a museum of my photography and poetry, along with quilts and drums.

Have had a profile written up in the Acadiana and Baton Rouge *Advocate* newspapers.

Was a guest speaker for a spiritual group in Kaplan.

Rented booth space at a vintage/arts and crafts store.

Developed long lasting friendships.

– Rita Vincent

Rita Vincent

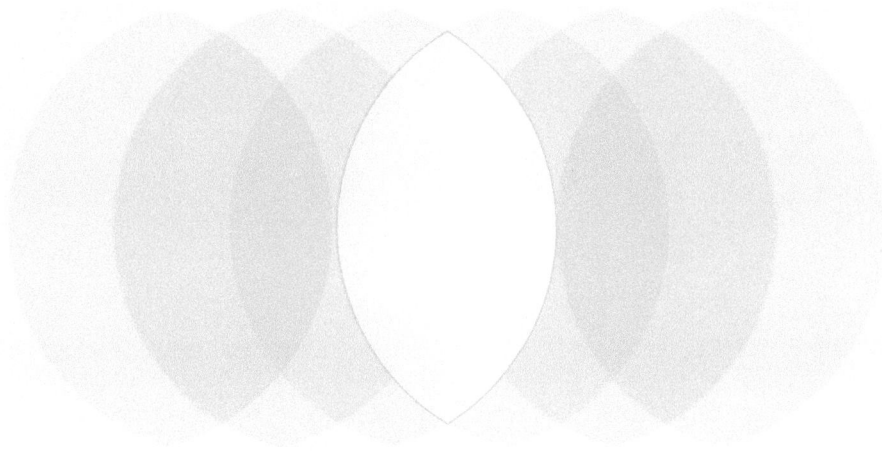

For me, the gift of The Heroine's Journey was to be supported by a group of women throughout the year. Through every change, through every loss, through all blessings, and through all of my accomplishments, these women stood by me as I journeyed through life. When I was encouraged to go to a drum circle to learn how to play the djembe, a Western African drum, my *Heroine's Journey* sisters urged me on. I practiced everyday and went to drum retreats and drum circles, and soon, I was good enough to join a local group. I performed with other musicians on stages in Lafayette and Austin. I started working in a store that sold only djembes, and I would play with the customers. I led drum circles at big churches in Austin. It was because of my circle of women that I learned to believe I could not only play the drum, but make a difference with it.

First, I played for the local halfway homes for women. When I saw how these abused and troubled women responded, I knew I was on to something. I took my drum into inpatient substance abuse clinics. The drumming reached men and women who had, before then, fiercely protected their emotions. Yet, the drumming was able to reach their hearts. I was then asked to work with inmates at our local jail. I began teaching the drum to mentally troubled inmates. Playing my djembe in this way enabled me to start a collection of drumming experiences that I now call "PrisonBeat." Since I started, I have shared my rhythms and encouraged others to find their own with nearly 300 people. Like me, they were struggling to find their place in the world. Where for some there was no hope, drumming has now allowed many to tap into their soul and find peace. I'm so grateful for *The Heroine's Journey* program. Each stage has been a stepping stone for growth. Each stone has had a song for me that I, in turn, share with others. I know my truth. *The Heroine's Journey* process and a great circle of women led me to the promise that I can do anything if I just believe in who I am. This has allowed me to bring joy and hope and lots of rhythm to those on the margins of society.

– Lee Ann Broussard

As I sit here in wonder
looking back on a year gone by
I feel a sense of warmth
and chills run through my veins

As I remember the sharing of hearts
the tears, the pain, the laughter
from six women I'd never met
our souls were immediately connected
along with the friend I'd already had

When I arrived I was strong and determined
I resented that I was imperfect and had to be here
As the months went by I endured "these" women
Thinking this was a waste of my time
Finally realizing this time was my salvation

I surrendered to the MARI
It released the past from haunting my soul
I embraced my pain, my loss, my fears
And my reward has been my peace

I thank the divine higher power
Who brought me my new found sisters
That have stood by me thru thick and thin
I celebrate the time I've spent with you
For you are the true heroines in my life!

– Judy Vaughn

Judy Vaughn

Elizabeth Carrington

We are seven women
traveling side by side.
Not alone but together
it has been an emotional ride.

Each an individual
hidden talents to unfold.
The support we show each other
provides a comfort to behold.

Within our sacred circle
This haven we gather to —
a space to share our deepest thoughts
with faith and gratitude.

At first, my heart is empty
I was feeling such despair.
With time, I feel much calmer now,
my fragile self repaired.

It is quite an honor
To be part of this.
On a soul filled journey
towards enlightened consciousness.

– Elizabeth Carrington

Savasana's got the 411

This morning, when I was quiet on my mat
trying to figure out if I was
          laying . . .
          or lying . . .
an enormous dove emerged from my throat.
          Not my mouth.
          My throat.
It exploded from a shaft of golden light.
The thundering of wings silenced
          the inhales
          and exhales.
The thundering of wings filled that little room.
          The wings of a bird.
          The feathers of the wings of a bird.
The feathers of the wings of a bird remind me of my father's hair.
Downy, golden layers with a lining of snowy white.
One hot tear broke the sweat on my cheek.

I realized later that I cried
simply because there had been a time
when I could touch my father's hair.

– Jane Blunschi

Jane Blunschi

Simone Simon

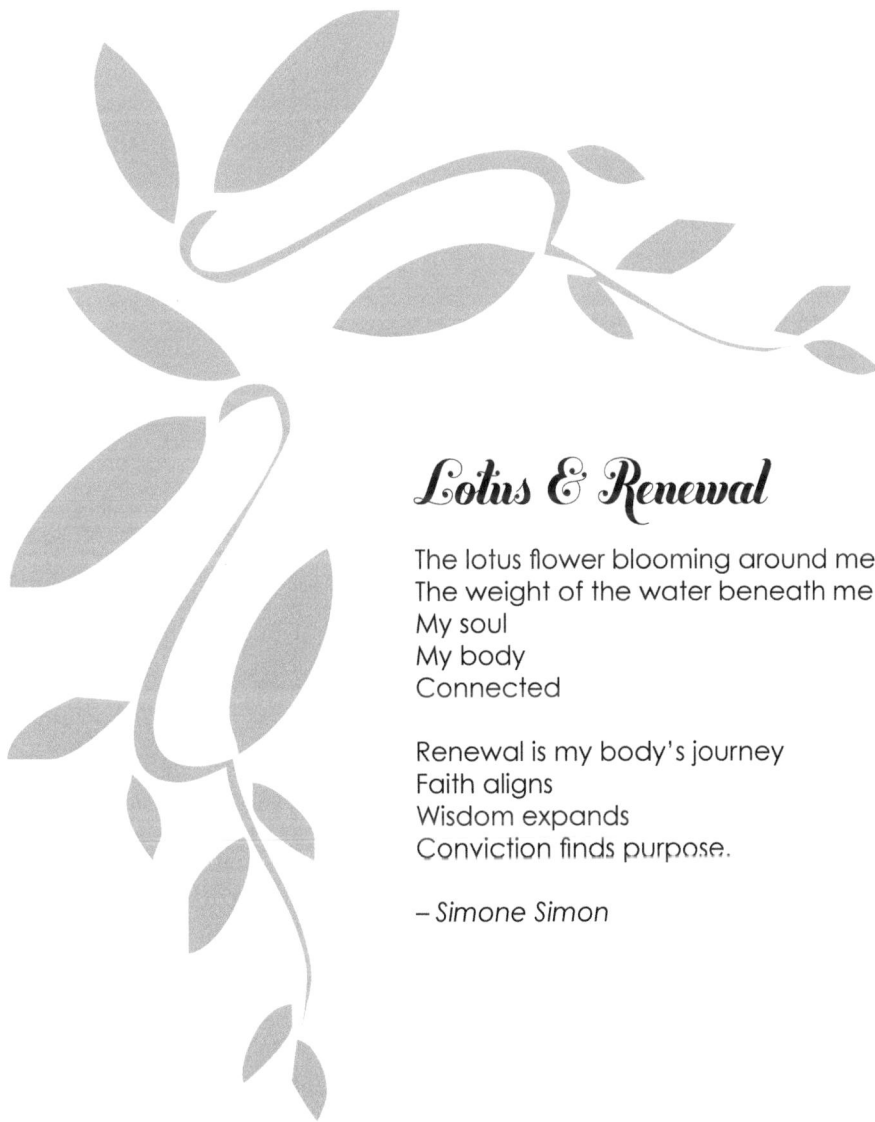

Lotus & Renewal

The lotus flower blooming around me
The weight of the water beneath me
My soul
My body
Connected

Renewal is my body's journey
Faith aligns
Wisdom expands
Conviction finds purpose.

– Simone Simon

Marjorie Bourgeois

I am the mother of 3 grown children
Who lives by herself in the country.
I do needlework, some arts, some crafts,
I also do yard work and spend time in my garden.

Last week, I returned a phone call at work,
I described myself as "The Physical Therapist"
And I listed the town in which I live.
That is who I have been for the last 32 years.

Now, I am committing suicide to that
Which I have created and have become.
The death struggle is fierce, as I have
Witnessed in others in hospitals and homes.

After the death of my clinic, what will
I do, where will I go, who will I become?
As I said, I am the divorced mother
Of three, who lives by herself in the country.

I came to this town selling oranges
Selling them on the street with other street people.
Six years later, married with 2 children, I became
The first woman to open a private practice in the area.

I have had many struggles and many joys.
I helped to integrate a KKK town
That was mandated to me after I left
St. Louis and the inner city in turmoil.

I have been allowed to sweat, work, and pray.
With my patients, I watched miracles happen.
I also have had my share of failures
And watched in despair when others failed.

I felt completely at home here in my town
Which is a blue collar town of hard workers.
They accepted me, an outsider, a previous
Seller of oranges on their streets.

My identity has been from many as follows:
"You're the one who helped my Mom or my Dad."
"You're the only one who knew what was wrong with me."
"You saved my life." "You helped me walk again."

Now as I close the door on who I have been,
I have terrible agony and pain in my gut.
I created something from nothing, I gave
It life, and we lived a spiritual life together.

Death comes when we are old, gray, and wrinkled.
Well, I am gray and wrinkled, but still alive.
Saying goodbye and feeling confused,
I sit and hold myself as the tears fall.

– Marjorie Bourgeois

Me, Maiden, Mother, Crone

It is I, it is me, standing before the fire, holding the past in my hand. My body aches, feeling flushed and tense.

It is me, the maiden, who appears to guide me as I rip apart the patterns that have so dominated my life.

It is me, the mother, who lovingly holds my hand, as the last of the patterns become but a memory.

It is me, the crone, who leads me to the cleansing waters and into the best part of my life.

– Marguerite Landry

The Heroine's Journey has been a deep and gentle transformational program that has assisted me in Being in the world. It has been the catalyst in shifting many relationships in my life in a very wonderful way. It has allowed me to sit with very brave and courageous women who continue to pursue their dreams. Many thanks to Fran Clarke for your beautiful wisdom and gentle guidance in this wonderful program.

– Melanie Robin

Beneth Arceneaux

Dragonfly

Through crisis there is growth

       But also Death
Some part of you changes.
      It DIES!

Resulting in defeat of
      Self created illusions.

Your eyes are OPENED!
      To the Gateway

A breakthrough
      powerful & poised

Death. We give Thanks

We grow — Mature —
A depth of character evolves

Transformation
      Of a New Light

Living "In" the Moment. NOW.
Sweet embrace

Normal

What are you?
Is it what is accepted?
Who determined you?
      My mother —
      My mother's mother —
      Or generations before
This I now question . . .
My eyes were closed but are now opened.

– Beneth Arceneaux

Dedicated to my Sister Heroines and women of all ages . . . present, past, & eternal.

There is a Divine essence of womanhood far beyond that of just giving life. Women are intrinsically designed, instinctively capable, and intuitively gifted to be resilient and powerful. It is through the duality of our capabilities — strong and enduring, yet graceful and nurturing that we have created and carried existence. This is our sacred truth. It is one buried deep within the very DNA of not only humanity, but Mother Earth herself. From the first spark of Divinity that ignited creation, it is woman that forms, shapes, and molds our 'Tree of Life.'

Our roots run deep within the earth carrying up generations of wisdom and experiences in order to nurture life. Woman forms the trunk of life's tree, giving stability and height necessary to withstand storms, providing nutrition to endure the path ahead. We are the branches that extend to all living existence here on earth to share in both joy and sorrow. As branches, we weave and intertwine because instinctively we know that bound as one collective we are stronger. Women are the leaves that gather, surround, and protect the fruit — our children — to ensure that another generation will survive.

– Chantelle Blanchard

Testimonials

Acceptance of my creative gifts. **Betty Landreneau**

Gaining a personal realization that who I am, and that I am is enough. I don't have to sell my soul to be loved and appreciated. I don't have to earn it. I am, therefore I am loved. **Bessie Senette**

The Heroine's Journey, Fran, and the women who committed to creating our circle provided a safe space for me to express my true self, to process the pain and sorrow of the journey, and to share my deepest desires; a nurturing container from which to begin the process of fully manifesting my life's purpose. I am indebted to my sister Heroines and to Fran. **Adrianne Smith**

It was so liberating to begin again. To unravel the threads of my life and reweave them into a new tapestry. I have discovered that I need no one else's permission except my own to reinvent myself. **Karen Simon Durio**

Watching each woman grow into her own independent being, a being who does not depend on others to make her happy. Knowing the signs of the cycles and spirals of life and death makes it easier to navigate the paths. I know that when that particular cycle ends, another particular cycle will begin. Which particular cycle is the mystery, but the cycles start to become familiar and one gains confidence going through them. It is a great feeling to be a Heroine and meet up with another Heroine along the path. **Tammy Labiche Henley**

Heroine's Journey, an initiation of sorts, was a crucial step onto my path of empowerment. Much gratitude to Fran, on behalf of myself and all women, for guidance and encouragement. **Denise Thibodeaux**

I learned to love and take care of myself (mind, body and soul). **Judy Vaughn**

Safety to self-explore. **Joy Merino**

Loving and accepting myself has been the greatest benefit of *The Heroine's Journey* thus far; I continue to grow with each of life's new experiences. **Denise Marceaux**

The Journey helped me regain my passion for life while excavating personal obstacles so that I could work to change what was not edifying to me. **Lee Ann Broussard**

Meeting amazing women and watching them grow! **Elizabeth Carrington**

Learning and becoming true to myself. **Brittany Broussard**

Learning that there are so many other strong women on the same journey of self-discovery right along with me, no matter our age, experiences, or background. **Katherine Moody McCormick**

We shared; we gave, but we did not take. We listened; we cried, but we did not judge. .....I am not alone on the journey! **Kandise France**

The Heroine's Journey connected me to my core being, introducing me to the divine which lies within, giving me the strength to heal. **Jessica Wiley**

The Heroine's Journey has given me the gift of self-awareness and the realization that my happiness lies in how I choose to react to the opportunities, events and obstacles life places in my path. **Angie D. Broussard**

The Heroine's Journey helped me accept myself for who I really am and to live my life by my expectations alone. I am not responsible for anyone's happiness except my own. **Lori Duval**

The benefit that continues for me is a profound appreciation of the importance of women's circles and an understanding of the power and magic of the Feminine in me, my community and the world. **Alyce Morgan Wise**

Personal transformation and self-growth on a consistent timeline created the opportunity to amass a large collection of work, and to access a deep and profound perspective of obstacles overcome and growth achieved - highly valuable work and worth the investment. **Stephanie McCullor**

The Heroine's Journey allowed my exploration into my authentic self. It allowed me to process, accept and learn from past experiences which have led to my growth in character and humility. This journey has transformed my thoughts. **Beneth Arceneaux**

Empowerment!! Through *The Heroine's Journey* and the guidance from Fran I was able to tap into something I haven't felt in years, if ever. Not only knowing that I'm ok being "me," but also knowing who "me" is! I no longer walk through life looking through the eyes of others. I have the freedom, the power and the strength to walk through MY life with my own eyes, following my own heart and not getting caught up in the crazy sense of perfection that doesn't exist. The Journey helped me release demons from my past so that I could live in the present. I am a better mother, wife, friend, sister, and daughter because of my walk on the Journey, I am a better ME! ~ "LIVE OUT LOUD, and be louder every day!" **Carmen Vidrine**

Thanks to *The Heroine's Journey*, I rediscovered who I truly am, deep down in my soul; this discovery strengthened my core. **Silvia Bertolazzi**

It supported, empowered and aligned me with my soul's purpose to be a full time artist. **Kathy Dumensil**

The Heroine's Journey changed my life. It gave me the permission I thought I needed to embrace and celebrate all of me. It allowed me the freedom to know and love the "saint" as well as the "sinner", the "little girl" as well as the "sexy gypsy", the "calm, wise mother" as well as the "wild, uninhibited woman" which are all the wonderful parts of me. My journey gave me a sacred place to just BE without judgment or expectations. It gave me the tools to face and embrace all of life with open arms and an open heart. My journey gave me the greatest gift I could receive... It gave me MYSELF! **Tracy Voisine**

To let go with love and dignity. **Robin Harbourt**

The awareness of my inner and outer creative uniqueness, and the knowledge that it is to be expressed and celebrated in whatever fashion I choose in the journey of life. **Linda Lolan**

Several of the activities within the program re-introduced me to the rhythmic parts of myself. **Jany Champagne**

The one greatest benefit of *Heroine's Journey* is having the opportunity to develop four trusting, dynamic, lifelong, worthy friends. With Gratitude . . . **Harriett Taylor**

The greatest benefit of The Heroines Journey was the bonding and growth of feminine souls through guided experiences. **Beverly Breaux**

The greatest benefit, for me, was the authentic connection made with the amazing women in my group. It is an awesome, life-giving, soul-sustaining experience to be so deeply seen and accepted and to have the opportunity to return that gift in kind. **Virginia Webb**

The Heroine's Journey is not a program, nor a path, nor a phase for me; it has become a way of life that I still follow today. **Marguerite Landry**

Being in a group of women open, willing and ready to accept change and growth was encouraging, and let me safely become my authentic self. **Lauren Dupre**

The greatest benefit of *Heroine's Journey* is awakening to an inner truth, a new awareness or purpose that is life-long and transformative. **Jess Breaux**

The Heroine's Journey was my first step towards a more authentic life. I discovered not only what it means to be a true individual, but a woman with her own voice and a spirit to discover. **Simone Simon**

The awakening of poetry in my life as an expression of my feelings and innermost thoughts. **Rita Vincent**

Heroine's Journey awakened some yet-unexplored region of my heart and life.
I better recognize and am grateful for the blessings of my rich relationships and creative spirit. I am more aware that my life is part of something divinely greater than I had imagined. My life is richer and more expansive for trusting the Divine Mystery that encouraged my *Heroine's Journey*. **Cheryl Guidry**

The greatest treasure is the insight into myself, a peaceful acceptance, and personal freedom. **Kathryn Vincent-Dore**

When I signed up for *The Heroine's Journey* I thought I would draw, listen to some music, and enjoy being creative with some smart women. It was so much more than that. It was like the difference between going out for a loaf of bread versus taking a trip around the world. It was slow and subtle but by the time we had our final session, I had moved a long way into facing personal fears, seeing my abilities, and knowing my own power. Sometimes I look at the art I made and find I am surprised again at all that was inside me, waiting to be discovered. Now when life sends me on journeys, I am more prepared to move forward with purpose, excitement, and curiosity. I am so grateful that I got a chance to do this process with Fran and a group of wonderful supportive women. **Linda Christian**

Inner knowledge and outer joy. **Marjorie Bourgeois**

Many women . . .

......Believe that they are powerless to affect change in their lives, resorting instead to passivity, complaining, blaming others for their lack of happiness or fulfillment.

............Are experiencing a general sense of malaise and loss of passion for life, diagnosed as depression and anxiety.

...................Are trying to find their life purpose.

..........................Do not know that what they believe to be true about themselves is only conditioned learning, and can be unlearned and replaced with life enhancing beliefs.

..............................Exist in relationships that are draining, demeaning, domineering, and abusive.

......................................Shape their lives trying to gain the approval of others.

....Have never known the transformative power of a circle of women committed to the intention to grow.

All of us contain the Divine spark of our creation. Though sometimes dimmed by experiences which imprint distorted perceptions of ourselves and the world, this soul spark, this spirit of life, always exists, awaiting our re-discovery. *The Heroine's Journey* program provides a template, a way to re-connect with our essence, a way to take responsibility for our lives by acknowledging and aligning with personal values. This program helps women to:

- Find answers to the question: Who am I?
- Re-discover buried passions.
- Make empowered choices in alignment with our truths.
- Have compassion for ourselves and others.
- Know our innermost drives, values, motives, and passions.
- 'Be' who we are rather than who we pretend to be.

Our life purpose is not found in a job or career. Our purpose is to live authentically, and from that place we can participate in service to others.

This is a time of unprecedented change in the world. Now, more than at any other time in recorded history, we have the responsibility to 'find our voices' and use them to help promote peace and harmony for all citizens of the planet. This starts by each of us doing personal inner work. We must first stop the wars inside ourselves and then with others. We contribute to peace in the world when we experience peace in ourselves. Every individual thought and action has a profound impact through the web of collective consciousness. War never brings peace; only love can bridge diversity and differences to foster peace — love for ourselves, love for others, love for the planet.

– Fran Clarke

FRAN CLARKE is dedicated to assisting women to open to the joy in their lives. She is the creator of *The Heroine's Journey: A Woman's Search for Truth*.

Her passion for engaging women is not limited to the U.S. as she is also the Founder of Yassah's Sisters, a program which assists women in rural Northern Liberia, Africa.

As an activist and advocate, she speaks her truth where it is needed and participates in peace-building initiatives that promote compassion and unity. She sees the world through the eyes of wonder and is continuously involved in the evolution of consciousness of herself and others.

Fran has been a psychotherapist for 25 years and has created a practice that incorporates sound, music, vibration, and energy psychology to foster personal transformation.

Her joys include experiencing foreign cultures, close personal friendships, the spirituality of music, beauty of nature, and two amazing adult children. She resides in a cottage in the country near Lafayette, LA.

For information on how you can participate in *The Heroine's Journey* or bring the program to your locale, please contact:
FRAN CLARKE
200 W. University Ave.
Lafayette, LA 70506
Office: (337) 235-1261
E-mail: ffclarke1@gmail.com
www.hellotolife.com

www.ingramcontent.com/pod-product-compliance
Lightning Source LLC
Chambersburg PA
CBHW041956100426
42812CB00018B/2662